WHY MISREAD A CLOUD

"In a dizzying and cinematic sequence, the prose poems that embody *Why Misread a Cloud* juxtapose images of war with the images of the everyday. Crucially accompanying these sensory moments of alarm are chasms of silence. What these jagged sequences and disruptions urge the reader to do is see that a cloud can transform into a fighter jet's contrail. And just like that, the roar of a sonic boom disrupts what has been taken for granted. Emily Suzanne Carlson's razor-sharp language urges us to look deeply at the contours of the sky and learn how, even at the edges of a peaceful horizon, there is the capacity for storm."

—Oliver de la Paz

"In these spare, bladed, sometime single-sentence, prose poems, Emily Carlson asks us not to let the curtain fall because, 'what we don't see, remains.' These are compassionate, but blistering, poems of witness that twine together the violence, injustices, and ruination of two wartime geographies: the 2006 Lebanon War and the United States police militarization in an historically Black neighborhood. From 'plumes of ash' to 'midnight ash' to 'wedding dress ash,' *Why Misread a Cloud* spotlights collapse while simultaneously providing an umbilical cord to hope, because amid fear and devastation, is a newborn as well as a child who simply states, "My favorite part of me are my eyes because they let me see the beautiful world."

—Simone Muench

"Beautiful and searing, the short prose poems of *Why Misread a Cloud* accrue like snowflakes against a fence, using their delicate weight to allow us to better see what's right in front of us. Grounded in body and place, they offer not so much an account as an experience: of the fragmented moments that assemble into histories; of the disorientation of violence as it plays out across cities, homes, people; of the way the I evaporates in stages under such conditions even as it persists, which means continues to exist. F16s interrupt an afternoon of coffee and cherries. Sound cannons blare behind an infant nursing. By one imperative or another, people are forced from their homes. Here, without losing their specificity, different violences are allowed to drift and merge, to reveal their sameness, as Emily Suzanne Carlson points us toward ours."

—Lisa Olstein

THE SUNKEN GARDEN AT HILL-STEAD MUSEUM

Sunken Garden Poetry began in 1992 in Farmington, Connecticut, with a single poetry reading in the magical setting of Hill-Stead Museum's Sunken Garden, drawing huge crowds even that first year. Since then the annual series has become one of the premiere and best-loved venues for poetry in the country, featuring the top tier of American poets as well as emerging and student writers from the region. From its inception more than twenty-five years ago, this poetry festival has given equal weight to the quality of text and the poet's ability to deliver an engaging, powerful, and entertaining experience in the unique theater of the Sunken Garden.

Out of the festival have grown competitions, year-round workshops and events, and an educational outreach to Hartford high schools. And while centered at Hill-Stead— with its beautiful views, Colonial Revival house, and priceless collection of Impressionist paintings—Sunken Garden Poetry now engages an ever-wider audience through a growing online presence; public radio broadcasts; and an annual chapbook prize, co-published by Tupelo Press.

THE SUNKEN GARDEN CHAPBOOK POETRY PRIZE

2022
Why Misread A Cloud by Emily Suzanne Carlson

"In brief paragraphs that are neither prose nor prose poems, we meet a witness. A speaker who is not in her country of origin. A person living in the air of violence. Militarization. And very occasionally, a mundane gesture–adding sugar to tea. The spareness creates a poetics that is, at once, elegantly stark and akin to journalism. We read between the lines because what is unsaid, makes this a poetry of image and association. What was once a broom for sweeping a kitchen, is used by a woman to sweep propaganda leaflets off the street. I find myself engaged in a place–to a place, really–where there are ballistic helmets. Yes, strange and strangely familiar. This is how art and dreams work: with the familiarity of knowing and the disassociation that can allow insight."

— from the Judge's Citation by Kimiko Hahn

2021
bed by Elizabeth Metzger
Selected by Mark Bibbins

2020
Salat by Dujie Tahat
Selected by Cornelius Eady

2019
Diurne by Kristin George Bagdanov
Selected by Timothy Donnelly

2018
Flight by Chaun Ballard
Selected by Major Jackson

2017
Ordinary Misfortunes by Emily Jungmin Yoon
Selected by Maggie Smith

2016
Feed by Suzanne Parker
Selected by Jeffrey Levine & Cassandra Cleghorn

2015
Fountain and Furnace by Hadara Bar-Nadav
Selected by Peter Stitt

2014
We Practice For It by Ted Lardner
Selected by Mark Doty

ISBN: 978-1-946482-79-2

Cover and text designed by Allison O'Keefe

Cover art: Albert Bierstadt (1830-1902), "Cloud
Study with Sea and Sky." Oil on paper.
Detroit Institute of Arts
First edition: November 2022

Tupelo Press

P.O. Box 1767

North Adams, Massachusetts 01247

(413) 664-9611 / Fax: (413) 664-9711

editor@tupelopress.org / www.tupelopress.org

Tupelo Press is an award-winning independent
literary press that publishes fine fiction, non-fiction,
and poetry in books that are a joy to hold as well as
read. Tupelo Press is a registered 501(c)(3) nonprofit
organization, and we rely on public support to carry out
our mission of publishing extraordinary work that may
be outside the realm of the large commercial publishers.
Financial donations are welcome and are tax deductible.

WHY MISREAD A CLOUD

Emily Suzanne Carlson

"What we have to do, then, is become *the Sun itself, so all fear of separation can forever be ended."*

–Rumi

*

In July 2006, I was on scholarship to study poetry in Lebanon when the war began. I believed I would survive the psychological effects—as long as I didn't see the tanks. The Merkava, Hebrew for "chariot," were made for long-range continuous bombardment, with self-propelled artillery that can fire without hesitation. I believed as long as I didn't hear their low rumble and the rattle of their track plates touching the earth, I wouldn't wake (though I did) sweat-drenched and screaming from nightmares for years afterward. I didn't see the tanks. From my balcony above the Mediterranean's blue-green, I saw the blockade by sea, warships lining the horizon. I saw fighter aircraft streak the sky and towers of ash in their wake. I saw attack helicopters descending upon anxious bathers on the beach, resisting the fear that kept us indoors. I saw the face of a gunner, a kid in his early twenties like me. Under their fire, the power plant exploded, plumes of ash and smoke filled the sky and ten million gallons of oil gushed into the sea. I didn't live on the shoreline. I had no children here. I had not, for all my life, loved the olive trees, the dew on their branches, the mountains rising from the sea.

I had not imagined that six years after I returned home to the United States, a tank would enter the historically Black neighborhood where my partner and I, both white, had our first child. The Department of Defense had further militarized the police, equipped them as an occupying force. Summer nights were studded with sirens and megaphones ordering our neighbors from their homes. As a white person, if I didn't intercede, I was safe. During pre-dawn raids on Dede's family's home, the SWAT team carried shields and enormous rifles; they knocked down the door, ordered everyone from their beds. When I leaned from my window to film, the turret on the tank pivoted, and the sniper shifted his rifle from their door to my face. But I needed only to let the curtain fall. My whiteness would protect me, as it did and does. I needed only to step away from the window. What we don't see, remains.

*

I saw from my balcony, warships in the sea, *you have to leave*, mother said into the phone, jets broke the sound, barrier, sonic booms meant, to sound like bombs, how not to mention it, midnight ash onomatopoeia, *who wants you to be afraid*, Fadi repeated, and added sugar to his tea

From my bedroom window I film the officers until the turret on the armored tank pivots. The sniper rifle aims at my face. "Move away from the window," says the megaphone. Floodlight washes color from the walls.

"I" evaporates in stages, showered, with my clothes on a, zero, in blanks, that bridge, a list of ways to stay, gone, the mouth of a tunnel, my own mouth,

Raids with armored tanks intensify. Officers
appear in camouflage, with vests and ballistic
helmets. Sound cannon, sonic weapon, LRAD,
some of these don't even have names— My baby's
lip quivers on my nipple and milk's warm stream
fills his mouth. But of their sound: "six decibels
per doubling distance," "geometric spreading"—

Sounds without names, light burst, into rooms, without its sea-facing wall, the building appeared a dollhouse, anyone could reach in, say, please pass the salt, unable to discern, what is what, a kettle's steam from F-16s, high heels on the stairs, an attack from the sea at the point of collapse, before this, what was an hour, coffee, cherries,

Police have broken the door to little Dede's house. Later, they arrive at the dollhouse. Dede's voice gone deep commands, "Party's over." With tenderness she lifts the dollhouse people from their beds and floats them out where there is no door.

Paper fell from the sky, from parachutes, fighter aircraft, artillery shells, one read, *We advise you to leave your homes, we are not responsible for the consequences if you ignore our warning!* elderly women, having seen it before, brought their brooms to sweep leaflets into the sea

The landlord posts rent-hikes, nails plywood over broken windows. My neighbor shakes her head, "I'm moving because I'm tired of it." Another morning, 30-day eviction notices appear on doors, blow across yards, sidewalks. Vouchers collect in storm grates. Later, someone pastes drawings of vultures to condos, where once vacant lots gathered rain.

You must immediately leave your villages for your safety.

No callers will be revealed the reward could be anything from cash to a new house!

The development company wants "to attract a new demographic." Their slogan, "The Place To Be."

A child puts it this way, "You'll have to go to a different school and leave all your friends and it'll just be a tough job for you."

Walking through a dark room I sensed where to step, adjusting the radio, it became clear, ash wasn't a storm, blown over the sea, goodbye sea, goodbye stars, why misread a cloud, that won't rain, that's ash, of what

In the garden, ballistic helmets, armored vests, a SWAT team in shields will not block what we are about to see.

What does nothing feel, like, is a sensation and all that, repeats

Would you call it war or invasion? My neighbors
empty-handed in the street in sweatpants and
nightgowns. Who will say what the charge was for.

Fadi turned from the news, when he saw me, and began to laugh a hand-over-the-mouth-laugh, jelly-legs-laugh, doubled-over-laugh, he had to lie down on the floor, at some point that afternoon, I had cut my hair, *What have you done, Mess America?* he asked *How will we fix this?* explosions, I could not, change but my hair

I carry my baby into the windowless hall. What if a stray bullet?

News reached elsewhere before us, *The evacuation has begun* my mother said over, the phone the runways bombed, the borders, if we left we had to leave by, sea, where whose ships arrive, to take whom away, whose evacuation, whose drinks on a silver tray, whose mountain, whose moon

Whose police vehicle to take who away.

From evacuation lines stepped a lone bride *You've made a shitpile of my dignity* whoever says that, isn't permitted to board the ship, Marines beckoned my white, her wedding dress ash, in the bombed airport, lifted me over razor wire closer to the sea, where do we store all this ruin, she asked me to say, *I'm with her* to raise my, yellow slip, a Marine shook his head, *The 1's circled that means you're alone*

The deputy shouts, "Put your hands in the air. Put your goddamned hands in the air." Out a window Marvin Gaye sings, *I need some lovin'*—

They say you have a window of time before the bombing intensifies,
my mother said

I did not ask, *how does one continue to face this?*

I could hear my body saying *I am just the body* and
within me space untouched

Police tape, broken glass. In the afternoon heat, drawing on the sidewalk, without turning away, a child says, "My favorite part of me are my eyes because they let me see the beautiful world."

From where we stand we wonder, *where's the light coming from*, over, a shattering, over and over—

ACKNOWLEDGMENTS

Gratitude to the Syria-Lebanon Nationality Room at the University of Pittsburgh for a travel grant which made this work possible. Gratitude to the editors and staff of *Aufgabe* for publishing an earlier version of "From the evacuation lines."

Deep bows of gratitude to Meg Shevenock and Robin Clarke for helping to bring these poems into being and, especially, for your friendship. To Joshua Zelesnick, Toi Derricotte, Joy Katz, Faith Barrett, Charlie Legere and the writing communities that have sustained me and this work. To my Borland Garden family for your reverence for the land and for one another. To the Olmo Ling community, especially Tempa Dukte Lama and Iris Grossman. To Gail Hunter. To Thomas Page McBee. To Fadi Melki, Rawad Saleh, Lynn Abdouni, and Sarah Abu-Zaid. To the children whose play and lives are inextricable from the life of this book especially Cyncere, Dede, Tracy, and Ja'Ron; and to my own children, Jules, Ravi, and Ocean. To my parents, Mom, Dad, and Cyndi. To my sisters Callie, Annie, and Taylor. To those working for racial justice, fair housing, and for peace.

Gratitude to Sten, all my love.

ABOUT THE AUTHOR

Emily Suzanne Carlson (she/they) is a mother, a poet, a teacher, and the director of Art in the Garden, a liberatory, anti-racist, LGBTQ+ welcoming, and joy-centered program that addresses the impacts of childhood adversity and trauma. Emily is the author of two prior collections: *I Have a Teacher* (Center for Book Arts 2016), and *Symphony No. 2* (Argos Books, 2015). Emily's writing has appeared in *Aufgabe*, *Bloom*, *Denver Quarterly*, *Fence*, *jubilat*, and elsewhere. Emily earned a BA from Sarah Lawrence College and an MFA from the University of Pittsburgh. With friends, they run the Bonfire Reading Series. Emily lives with their partner and their three children in an intentional community centered around an urban garden in Pittsburgh, Pennsylvania.